German Paradise Mallorca

German Paradise Mallorca

A Funny Telling

Illustrated with photos

Martin von Muenchen

THE HERMIT KINGDOM PRESS
Cheltenham • Seoul • Bangalore • Cebu

German Paradise Mallorca: A Funny Telling

ISBN 1-59689-003-7

Write-To Address:

The Hermit Kingdom Press
3741 Walnut Street, Suite 407
Philadelphia, PA 19104
United States of America

Info@TheHermitKingdomPress.com

Hermit Kingdom
12 South Bridge, Suite 370
Edinburgh, EH1 1DD
Scotland

http://www.TheHermitKingdomPress.com

"The song leads me, and strange beasts
guileless surround me, accustomed to serve;
I acknowledge them as creatures of my destiny
gentle to the fire and savage to portents."

Catalan Poet Carles Riba (1893 – 1959)

Contents

Introduction

What would be the best word to describe Mallorca? It's like asking a French man to describe wine. There are so many effusive adjectives that we Germans can use. But if you put a gun to my head and force me to pick one word, I will have to go with the popular German word, "spitze!"

Ja, Mallorca ist total grossartig! Of course, you have to go and experience it for yourself to get the total picture. But I will do my German best to give you a picture of the German paradise.

And it is my pleasure to share with you because Mallorca is simply spitze. It should not be hidden under the table. Put it on top of the kitchen table, I say. All should "see" it.

You will surely agree with me after reading this book. Ja, ich bin richtig. You will see that this mission had to be accomplished. Someone had to divulge the happy place of Mallorca. It's been going on for many, many days. Year in and year out, there have been millions of Germans who have partaken the magical waters of Mallorca. But the story has not really been told.

This paradise has been kept under water, like yellow rubber ducky on a bath tub filled with soapy water. Ja, that must not be. The story has to be told. And I will be the very one who will give you the fruit from the tree of knowledge.

You can take a big bite out of the apple. And you will know about the joys of the paradise. You may even feel like you have experienced a bit of that paradise. The best thing about this apple consumption is that you won't be kicked out of the paradise.

Ja, you heard me. It's what I would like to call "guilt-free consumption." So, take a piece of the juicy apple and let the juices run inside you and feel warm all over.

I am giving you the apple of knowledge. Ja, I am fulfilling a sense of duty to mankind. You will thank me for the telling. So, sit back and take a bike ride up to German paradise. Leave your familiar streets behind and follow me in a wonderful journey.

But before continuing on with this book, get up, go to the refrigerator, take out the big jug of iced tea or lemonade, and pour yourself a big one. Better yet, in a truly German fashion, get yourself a beer. Bier ist spitze!

The Setting

Ja, first things first. Where is Mallorca? Before I answer this question, let me confess to you something.

I wondered if I should describe the physical location of Mallorca. There are several reasons for this. I figure everyone should know where it is. I know in my mind that many people do not know where it is. Obviously, I know this to be true. If everyone knew where Mallorca is, then they would know what it's like. And if they all knew, then I would not feel the compunction to write this book. But you understand. In my heart, I feel that everyone should know where it is.

Secondly, I was a bit afraid that I would take away the special quality of the paradise. Describing its location and giving you the mundane details could bring the paradise down to the ground. And I want to keep the paradise high above the heavens. Ja, I want the German paradise to be special. It's such a spitze place.

But I know that I will have to overcome such a sentiment. For, I am here to show you German paradise. And it is important for you to know. Knowing where it is and other ordinary data will enhance your fantastic journey into the German Paradise. Ja, this has to be so.

So, where is this German Paradise? Mallorca is located in Spain. Yes, the country that has given the world Christopher Columbus and tapas provides the paradise for Germans.

Mallorca is an island. Floating happily in the warm waters of the Mediterranean, Mallorca is the biggest of the Baleric Islands. There are four of them: Mallorca, Ibiza, Formentera, and Menorca. The capital of these islands is Palma, and it's located in Mallorca.

In other words, you have access to the best services in the area. For instance, if you party hardy too muchy and you are in need of medical help, then the best hospital in the area is right there. You need other municipal services for whatever reason? No problemo. You need travel-related help? You have best services available to you. You want to experience what it is like to be a Spanish person? Ja, you can experience that too.

In a sense, you have the best of all the worlds. And you know us Germans. We don't like to take too many risks. We are Germans, for God's sake. We like things orderly. We like to plan things. We want to be prepared for when things go wrong. We want to be systematic. Ja, these are stereotypes. But it's true. We are Germans and we want order even in our paradise. And Mallorca provides this. Mallorca is truly a German Paradise.

I should give you a bit more info about this German Paradise. Mallorca is located in Catalunya. Ja, Catalunya is akin to saying "The South" in America. Catalunya enjoys proud traditions and history. But unlike the

South, there is a completely separate language (some would say "dialect"), called "Catalan." And Catalan has its body of literature and theatre. In fact, today, Catalan is the region's official language once again.

People of Catalunya are proud of their language and heritage in much the same way Irish nationalists are.

In Ireland, English is spoken everywhere, but high schools teach Irish, a Celtic language. In Catalunya, people speak Spanish, like the rest of Spain, but if we translate their pro-

Catalan sentiment into English, it would be something like: "Dang it! Ain't gonna forget no Catalan. It's what we are!"

The most famous Catalan city is Barcelona. Anyone who has visited Barcelona knows what a wonderful city it is. Certainly, Barcelona does not play second fiddle to Madrid.

Although you may want pure decadence of German Paradise, I would recommend making time to see Barcelona. You need at least a week to see the marvellous city and all that it has to offer. Certainly, check out Gaudi's works. The fundamentalist Catholic has produced some of the world's most beautiful architectural masterpieces.

I do have a bit of bad news, though. Although the proud people of Mallorca speak both Catalan and Spanish, they are not trilingual, normally. What does that mean?

If you are an Americano wanting to prance or strut your stuff around Mallorca, you will have to be ready to receive blank stares at your questions posed in English.

Now, don't go all judgmental on them, now. It's not like they need English for every day life. And why should they spend time away from the wonderful waters of Mallorca to humor some tourists, whom they will maybe meet in summer.

It's true, the younger generation sees more and more people speaking English. But not by much. So don't go expecting people to speak English to you. And don't get all mad and puffy if Spanish people you meet don't speak English. Don't forget, you are a tourist in their land and their language is Catalan and Spanish.

Okay, that's enough preachy preaching. But it's important. I feel as a German that I need to emphasize the importance of cultural sensitivity. If I say so myself, Germans make an effort to respect other cultures. We do. Ja, sicher!

Don't let der Fuhrer brainwash you from behind his grave. That period is like a botch of perfectly good painting. It's like someone else opening your bottle of wine via accident. Ja, forget der Fuhrer.

I am here to say that Germans are culturally sensitive. So, as a German, I feel like I need to share my sensitive side. Ja.

Coming from a country with somewhere between 3 million to 6 million Turkish people, it's clear why Germans are culturally sensitive.

And unlike the French, Germany never passes laws saying that Muslims cannot wear the religious headgear in public institutions. Ja, we Germans are tolerant and respect other cultures.

Even during the Nazi era, look at the allies we made a military pact with - Japanese people and Italians. For all the talk of Aryanism, we were quite tolerant of different countries, cultures, and races in many ways.

Okay, I guess I can let my German pride stop running like the cold beer freely running from its barrels in Mallorca. What I mean to say, of course, is that I would gladly have that beer not stop running. But I guess I have to stop drinking beer long enough to tell you about the wonderful German Paradise.

But you go sipping your German beer as you read this book. Is it Weissbier? White beer? It's great beer. It's all over Germany and you can find it in Mallorca, the German Paradise.

But it's not easiest to find in a typical bar in America. You can find German beer in German areas, like Wisconsin and parts of Ohio. If you live in these areas, drink some white beer and prost it to mich. Ja?

Ja, ich liebe Weissbier! And you will too, if you haven't tried it yet and try it. But do stay clear of banana white beer. That stuff is popular in Ravensburg in the southern part of Germany. But it's simply awful . . . .

I should probably give you some details about the weather. Ja, it's grossartig there in the German Paradise. Very sunny and very hot, like all the scantily clad German women at the beach.

Don't hate Germans because we are beautiful. Ja, German women are the best in the world. What is it that Americans say? "Gentlemen prefer blondes." Ja, and we have many blondes in Germany.

The German Paradise is, in fact, covered in blondes. So, gentlemen must love it there. Ja?

The best time to go to the German Paradise is in July or August. First of all, that's when the beaches are most concentrated with beautiful German women.

Less importantly, that's when it rains the least. Ja, you have those sporadic rain running through the beaches like a Frenchman chasing after a tall blonde German woman. But like the unsuccessful Frenchman (German women don't like Frenchmen at all because they think they are too wussy), wussy rains stop and let the powerful sun come back in like the proud Germanic tribal armies marching through France in ancient Roman Empire times and pouncing on the wussy French.

An umbrella is not necessary. Pack an extra suntan oil instead. Of course, if you are wussy French, you may need to bring an umbrella.

But the wussy French should bring emotional umbrellas for all the rejections they'll get from tall, leggy, French-hating German Frauleins. Ja, what can you say? Frenchmen are Frenchmen. They have never been liked by German women. That'll change when the Almighty comes back in the Second Coming. Ja.

What other practical info about the setting can I give? Money. Ja, I should say something about money. No more Spanish money. Spain uses the Euro, like the French and the Germans.

For Americans who may not know what Euro is, it is a currency created by Western European countries to make trade easier.

My biggest complaint in giving up the German Mark is that the new money looks like Monopoly money. Like some board game money. It's - what can I say? - wussy. The French probably like the wussy pictures on the Euro. But me, I'm a proud German. Give us money that looks like money, I say!

Despite the wussy, French-like pictures on the currency paper, Germans do generally like the idea of the Euro. We have been trying to unite Europe for centuries. What do you think the Third Reich was all about?

No, I'm not saying, resurrect Hitler. Hitler was Austrian, any way. Not really German.

I'm saying that Germany is the dominant power in Europe and having a single currency benefits Germany the most. I think Germans all implicitly know this and that's why we support the Euro so much. Deutschland über alles!

You have to excuse me. I am riding the new wave of German nationalism.

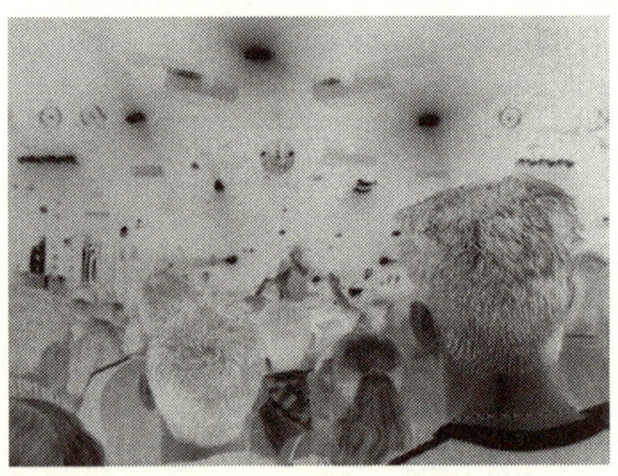

But it's good to see after years of being ashamed to be German. Some thought "German" meant evil. Nein! Nein! Nein! Germans are a good Volk!

I am proud to be German. And you will see many in the German Paradise now who are very proud to be German.

So, if you don't like Germany, you probably don't want to be wandering into the German Paradise. But if you do love Germans, you are in for a treat!

Paradise Beach

The best part of the German Paradise is the beach. Mallorca has great beaches.

Miles and miles of white sandy beach can be had in Mallorca. There is a reason why the Spanish royal family likes to spend their vacation in Mallorca - some royal fun in the sun, shall we say? And it's not like what Americans like to say, "Royal pain in the ass." The Spanish royal family is well liked by Spanish people and certainly welcome in Spain.

And it was the white sandy beach that attracted the Germans, culminating in what we now have as the German Paradise.

Let's face it. For red-blooded, heterosexual males, tall German women with sexy bodies contribute to the reality of the German Paradise.

Ja, German fraulein make you start singing at the top of your lung, "Pump it up!" or "Jump." Ja, you feel like saying, "Deutschland über alles!" And you are not even German.

Don't get me wrong. I don't like all the ideas associated with Aryanism. But it is hard to deny that there is something genetically superior about German women.

It's like God in Heaven picked out a chosen race to embody female beauty and the task has been entrusted to Germany.

Ja, I am proud of Germany. Ja, I am proud to be German. But I don't think that my pride clouds my vision. Any red-blooded heterosexual can see, German women as a group have far more genetically superior browny points than a randomly selected number of women from any other country. Ja, Gott sei Dank! Gott sei fricken Dank with generous helpings of Rum and Raisin ice cream.

What makes German women gift of God to mankind? Self-explanatory, nein? But allow me to indulge my gratitude to Gott im Himmel.

We Germans have the greatest concentration of blondes in the world, I am willing to bet. Ja, for men around the world, German women equal beautiful blondes. Nein? Do I not speak what is generally understood to be true?

And it is no joke. There are a lot of blondes in Germany. It's like God picked Germany to win the lottery for the most number of blondes.

German blondes are appreciated around the world. A blonde woman in Italy can be assured of being pinched in her cute, little blonde butt when she descends in her blondeness in Italy. And we all know that Italian men appreciate beautiful women.

It's like a flock of seagulls descending on a bratwurst meat fallen out of the oval white bread which enfolded it moments before. With alacrity they eat to their satisfaction. Ja, that's how it is when a German blonde walks down a street in Roma.

And it's not just Rome. It can be anywhere. These blonde German beauties can be big in Japan. Hip in Tel Aviv. Cool even in London. Ja, German blondes are great.

And it's not like only non-Germans like German women. German men are highly aware of the blessing from Gott in Himmel. God of Heaven has given us superior women and we show our appreciation in our own German ways. Ja, Gott sei Dank!

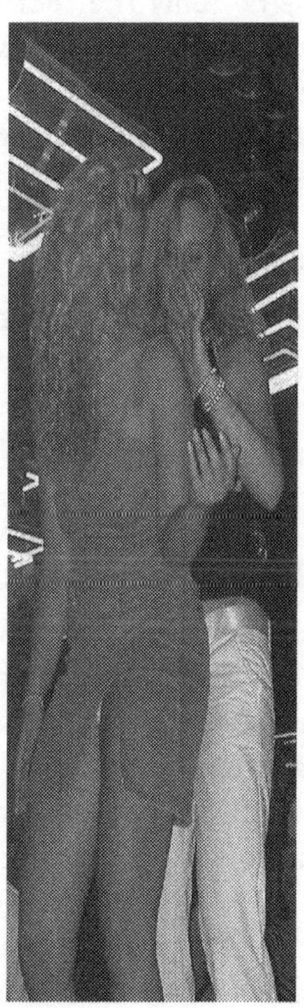

Ja, it is German men's appreciation of German women that propels us towards the German Paradise.

It is not only the fact that German women are blonde beauties that make German women special. What I call the German Women Character, or GWC, is certainly an important part of the package.

What are German women like? As a German dude, I have lots of comments on German dudettes. Ja, I know that German women are our crowning achievement as a Volk.

But before raving and raving about the merits of German fraulein, I will be honest and say some things that are critical. Ja, as perfect and exquisite as German fraulein are they have faults. Don't we all? We all have faults. Ja, das ist richtig!

First of all, German fraulein do not know what they want. Ja, das ist richtig. They change their minds all the time. It is ein bischen frustrating. Ja, any man who's dated a German fraulein knows what I am talking about. German fraulein are indecisive. Or, rather, they are decisive, but they change their decisions all the times. It's confusing. It's like a white mouse running back and forth as you dangle a piece of cheese from the air and move it left and right. German fraulein do not know what they want.

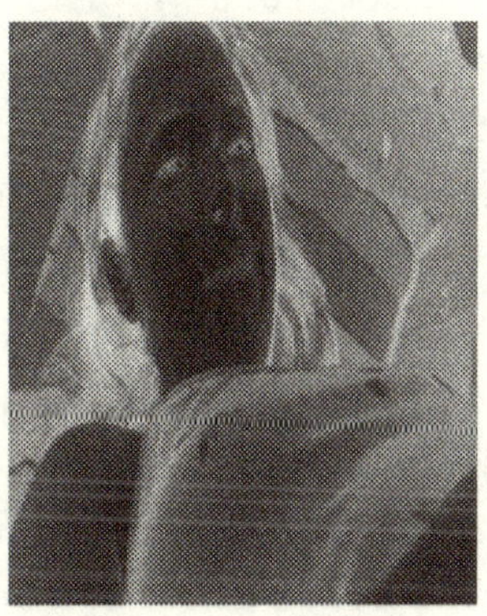

Ja, German fraulein change their decisions all the time. It is ein bischen annoying. If they were not beautifully blonde the way they are, all of Germany will go mad. Ja, whole Deutschland will disintegrate into nothingness because German fraulein keep changing their decisions.

But as I say, German fraulein are superior. Ja, they are. And that's why we German men tolerate their chaos. And I have to say they have many, many redeeming features. Ja, das ist richtig.

To start, German fraulein are gorgeous. Ja, das ist richtig. German fraulein are gorgeous in ways that the whole world knows it.

You ask, how does this relate to GWC (German Women Character)? Ja, that's a fair question. And I am ready to answer that. I surely am as I am one hundred per cent German who loves the Vaterland. I am ready to defend my Vaterland and the German fraulein who serve as its symbol. Ja.

Let's see it this way. Beauty is power. Ja. German fraulein are gorgeous and they know how to use it. When a German fraulein wants you, you do not stand a chance. You will fall comfortably in her hands like a duck jumping gracefully into a pond filled with water lilies. Ja.

German fraulein are not like wallflowers waiting for the man to go make the move. German fraulein are always moving like a battleship advancing towards its target. Like a U-boat ready to sink everything in sight in order to reach its goal. It may have something to do with the German character as grounded in warrior German tribes in the time of the Roman Empire.

Ja, German fraulein are something very, very special. Ja, that shows the power of GWC (German Women Character). Using what you have effectively to get what you want.

Ja, German fraulein are determined. They know how to use their resources. And they will achieve their goals.

German fraulein are not passive, as if the future is like a roaring lion and they are helpless sheep. No bah, bah!

Another GWC that brings honor to the Vaterland is boldness. German fraulein are like European Amazons.

Physical traits are certainly a good start to contribute to the image. Ja. German fraulein are tall and big. They are not puny and weak-looking. Being tall has its advantages in contributing to the Amazon-factor.

German fraulein tend to be tall. Tall and blonde. Magnificent fortresses built to stand all adversity.

German fraulein are like a castle built with large stones brought up the hill by hundreds of people. Like labor of love that realized a castle that stands centuries, Gott im Himmel took care and effort to construct German fraulein.

Ja, I believe in Gott. I believe that Gott exists because I see German fraulein.

No chance could have produced so many exquisite beings. It is Gott. Gott created German fraulein as His crowning achievement.

German fraulein have stature that is unparalleled. They are like the mythic Amazonians. They are magnificent! They are glorious!

With a physical stature of the Amazonians, German fraulein have their attitude as well. German fraulein are bold. German fraulein are fearless. German fraulein are programmed by nature to be leaders.

German fraulein are bold so that they are fun to be with. German fraulein will be found trying out salsa dancing, techno dancing, hip hop dancing. German fraulein do not care that they look ridiculous. They are bold and they are not going to pay attention to appearances.

In the context of the party scene, that is a credit. Ja. You can expect German fraulein to be fun and adventurous. You can suggest fun ideas and expect German fraulein to be willing to check it out.

German fraulein boldness is particularly evident when it comes to debunking normative social trends. Social expectations are often ignored by German fraulein if happiness is a goal. They learn to wade through the high tides to get to where they need to get to. Ja. It's simply impressive.

Ja, it is impressive. The boldness of German fraulein stands as a testimony to GWC.

The physical qualities coupled with GWC make German fraulein a crucial ingredient for the German Paradise. In fact, without German fraulein, Mallorca would not be a German Paradise.

It is like saying zebra is not a zebra without its stripes. It is like saying that an apple tree is not an apple tree without apples dangling from its branches in season. It is like saying a football game is not a football game if a football is nowhere to be seen. Ja, das ist richtig.

It's marvellous to have so many German fraulein in the German Paradise. Every heterosexual male cannot feel tempted but to kiss the hallowed ground of Mallorca in summer time. The German Paradise.

And German fraulein color the vast sandy beach of the German Paradise in their German glory. There is absolutely no dearth of gorgeous German fraulein; they come in droves in chartered planes from all over Germany. And they can be found happily frolicking on the sandy beach of Mallorca.

And the Paradise Beach is magnificent. Miles and miles of white stand. Miles and miles of clear, blue waters.

Warm waters of Mallorca beckon like the flashing adds in Time Square or Piccadilly Circus.

Like florescent neon lights in Tokyo, the glorious beach of Mallorca calls out to all to come and enjoy. There is so much fun to be had. There is so much to experience. The Paradise Beach.

There are many fun diversions to be had on the Paradise Beach. There are various water sports available.

You can find an inflatable object to float on in the water as you stare at the endless beach. Or you can, as many Germans do, participate in a group floating activity.

My favourite is floating on a boat. Jet boats are fun as they speed down the waterway and pass everyone by in a blink of an eye.

But my favorite is the banana boat. It's big, yellow boat that you can ride as a group.

It's what I call, "the group joy-ride." And Gott im Himmel, the way that boat moves through the waters, piercing the waves, as liquid squirts all over, it's quite an experience.

The exhilaration of warm wetness touching your very skin, mixing with hot sweat induced by sun pouncing on your tender skin, is sure to give you an ecstatic experience like no other.

And the boat travels fast. Gott im Himmel! It drives through fast and furious like ancient Roman chariot dashing through enemy lines.

The boats cuts through the wetness of the waters and you feel like you become one with nature. Ja, das ist richtig. It is absolutely incredible.

You have to experience it to know what I mean. But I hope I can give you a picture of the ecstasy of the group banana boat ride. Ja. Simply spitze!

Wrap you legs tightly around that boat like you would a wild horse just broken in. For you know, if you do not squeeze her body tight with your legs, she might bolt and you might fall.

Ja, treat the banana boat like you would a wild horse. And the wild horse will give you nothing but great fun.

Ja, wetness all around. Fun to be had. What is to complain about as you ride the waves on the banana boat?

But if you prefer a more tame experience, there are other types of boats available as well.

You can take it nice and easy and ride a group paddling boat. Ja, more exercise is involved to be sure.

Unlike the banana boat where you sit and enjoy, with paddling boat you have to move your body.

Ja, some real action involved here. But it's not just work. It is work resulting in pleasure. Immense pleasure.

Ja, move your body. Move your legs. And get the cycle going. And you will be rewarded with a ride of a life time. As you paddle and paddle, you will push through the wetness of the vast ocean. You will feel salty sweat of the sea dripping against your body.

You will feel tingly sensation like your body has been tenderized and your hormones naturally increased. Your bodily enzymes rushing through your body ready to go out - to explode in a pleasure attack.

Ja, you paddle and paddle. Paddle hard. Paddle hard. And you will go through the wet waters like a rocket flying through the heavens. Ja, totally spitze!

And you can slow your paddle. Go nice and easy. Slowly push through the water, feeling the lingering wetness on your body. Ja, the pleasure sounds of splashing waters audible and poignant. You can savor the joy of a slow paddle.

It's quite fun if you mix the speed routine. Go hard, then go soft. Push vigorously, then let loose. Push and push and then relent your push. Alternate your paddling patterns. Ja,

you can get maximum pleasure this way. Das ist richtig!
What can I say? Ja, it's an experience. Ja, good experience.

One word of advice. Make sure that you make your toes nice and firm as you paddle. With hard, fast toes, paddle that paddle like there is no tomorrow. Ja, push your leg against the paddle with hardened toes. That's a very important word of advice to get the maximum effect. Ja.

Physical exertion on a paddle boat can be deeply gratifying. You will burn a lot of calories. Sweat will be drenching the salty airs. Ja.

But you don't have to exert yourself if you don't' want to. There are other ways to enjoy a boating experience in the German Paradise.

You can take a sailboat out into the deep waters and go fishing. Get a fishing pole and see which fish you can catch. There are a lot of pretty fish in the sea.

Maybe you can make some music as you fish. As the sailboat gently rock back and forth. Let the fishing pole do the work.

Ja, it can be quite an experience. The boat rhythmically moving back and forth. Normalized motion like a train on a nicely designed train tracks can be quite pleasurable.

You can just lie back as your fishing pole plunges its line into the depths of the ocean. You can feel the heat of the sun on your chest, burning and burning, in a pleasurable sensation as your fishing rod explores the bottom of the ocean depths.

Ja, just let the boat rock back and forth. You can feel the water moving back and forth on your boat. Ja, the rhythm. It's quite something! Ja, das ist richtig!

But who says that water fun can be had only on a boat? Ja, there are many ways to enjoy the rocking of the ocean waves in the German Paradise.

Take for instance, various inflatable floatables. Ja, you heard me richtig. Ja, inflatable floatables can be quite pleasurable.

You know that the inflatable will float on the water with all the air blown into the tubes. Ja, hot air blown into the cavities can keep the blown inflatables puffy for a long time floating on the vast wetness.

There are various types of floatables to be sure. The most basic floatable is the doughnut floatable.

Doughnut floatables are great. You know warum? Ja, I will tell you. It is a pleasure to recount to you the pleasures of the doughnut inflatable. Ja, wirklich!

Just like a nice doughnut with a nice hole in the middle is inviting, the circular inflatable floatable with hole in the middle beckons to partake. Ja, das ist richtig.

When you see a nice doughnut, your mouth starts watering and you just want to bite into the soft but firm morsel. Ja, you just feel like sinking your teeth gently in and tasting the texture and the sweetness.

Ja, your mouth may not necessarily water as you gaze upon a quarter-bounceable floatable, but you will be eager to use it to experience the wetness of the vast ocean. Ja, das ist richtig.

Ja, the circular inflatable with a hole in the middle is spitze! The best thing about it is that you can put your body inside it as you float happily in the wetness of the vast ocean. Ja, it's something!

Ja, gently slide your body through the hole made for the purpose. Ideally, it will be a tight fit. Tighter the better, I say. Ja, tighter the better. Ja, it's so because you don't want your body to be too loosely inside the hole. You will keep slipping out. Ja, das ist richtig. Tighter the hole, your body will fit firmly in and your body will be held there as you bound up and down against the wetness of the rhythmic waves. Ja, it's something!

Ja, loose is not as fun. It's like wearing a loose shoe. Your toes will be slipping all over the place, and you can even slip and fall. Ja?

In other words, loose tube is like wearing pants that's two sizes too big. Your legs feel like they are running in an empty void - kind of like walking on the moon without gravity. Ja, das ist richtig.

Tight is good. Ja, das ist richtig. Tighter the better, I say.

I should say a few things about the logistics for a pleasurable tube-ride. The best way to get into the hole in the tube is to wait until you have walked a bit into the water. Carry the tube until you reach the water and put the tube down.

This way the tube will become nicely lubricated in the salty waters. Ja, the tube will be nice and wet for you to slide into. Especially if the tube is nice and tight, which is the ideal, you would want it to be naturally lubricated by the salty waters of the sea.

Feel the wetness of the tube. Feel the wetness of the insides of the tube with your fingers. When it is nice and wet with natural waters of the sea, slide right into that wet hole. Push yourself through the hole. Ja, completely inside the hole should your body squeeze through until you are on top of the tube and you feel the warm wetness below. Ja, be one with the paradise waters through the tight hole in the tube. And let yourself float back and forth through the rhythmic rocking of the waves.

There are other types of inflatable floatables as well.

Perhaps, the most popular kind is the rectangular floatable. Ja, these floatables are long - even to the length of a tall blonde German fraulein body. They can be exceedingly firm like the body of a German fraulein tennis player. Or they can be soft and fluffy like the body of a German fraulein swimmer. Ja, not all rectangular floatables are created equal. But then not all prefer the same kind of floatable. There is something for everyone. Ja, das ist richtig.

The best thing about these long inflatables is that they are multi-purpose. Ja, das ist richtig.

You can lie on their soft, fluffiness on the sandy beach as you feel the gentle breath of nature in your face. You can hear the sweet whispers of the German Paradise as your body presses against the inflatable. You can ease quietly into a pleasurable slumber as you feel the warm gaze of the summer sun on your face. Your floatable can be the perfect companion to your sleep-on-the-beach in the German Paradise.

And when you wake, you can take your long inflatable floatable for a rigorous swim.

The best thing about floating on the Mallorca waters with the long rectangular floatable is that you can do so much with it.

You can hold onto the inflatable floatable like you would a log freshly chopped down from the Rocky Mountain floating down a long river. You can paddle like a frog holding onto a piece of leaf fallen from a tall tree in a pine forest. You can give yourself as much exercise or none at all.

You can just lie on top of the inflatable floatable with your body fully extended floating on the waters of the German Paradise. You can lie with your face towards the heavens and let the sun grab you with her burning hot intensity as you become more and more enraptured in the glorious heat of summer. Or you can lie with your body towards the inflatable floatable, wrapping your arms tightly around its body as you press your whole being against the length of its slippery being. You will experience the pleasure of the floatation as your face is kissed all over by the salty waters of the German Paradise.

Just don't forget to deflate the floatable before leaving the beach, especially if you are intending to get on the bus. There is nothing as annoying as someone carrying a big inflatable floatable onto the bus when the bus is crowded. Deflate the hot air. Just remember bring the size down to form. That will keep everyone happy in a crowded bus. And yes, buses can get quite crowded.

Splashing fun in the waters is a lot of fun to be sure. Ja, das ist richtig. All the water sports can be nice, but sometimes it can detract from appreciating the wonders of the Paradise Beach.

German Paradise is what it is because it has miles and miles of beautiful sandy beach. It's like a gift from Gott im Himmel. It's simply marvellous. One cannot but just remain in awe and stare in amazement at the long stretch of beautiful, white sandy beach. Paradise Beach.

There is so much sand and so much beach space that millions of tourists who descend upon the German

Paradise is not enough to fill it. There are even more isolated, secluded areas available if that is more to your taste.

Ja, the German Paradise is basically all about miles and miles of beautiful beaches to cater to every taste. Ja, Paradise Beach is spitze!

The best thing about the Paradise Beach is that there are comfortable amenities for those who want it. There are ready chairs and aesthetically pleasing shaded areas for those who don't want to be burned to a crisp. Ja, some of us Germans have very pale, sun-adverse skins. Why become a lobster when it's more fun to eat lobsters?

Ja, the Paradise Beach is magnificent. All the beaches in the German Paradise are Paradise Beach. Sicher!

There are so many places to plop yourself down and enjoy the scene that the whole island is German Paradise. Every inch of it. Ja, das ist richtig!

Even when it is cloudy, Paradise Beach shows why it is a part of the German Paradise.

And the bad weather never lasts too long. A thunder shower will last something like 10 minutes and soon afterwards, it'll be sunny again.

It's like magic. In Germany, when it rains, it rains. Sometimes, it rains for days and days.

But in the German Paradise of Mallorca, the rain is there only to remind us how lucky we are to be in the German Paradise. A teaser rain shows the greatness of the sun and its warmth.

The German Paradise is so wonderful and the Paradise Beach so magnificent that you almost feel like you need a lifeguard to stop you from enjoying the paradise too much.

It's like a kid in a candy store with a free card to get whatever he wants. He may simply go mad. And that's how it is in the German Paradise. It's like overabundance of great things. Ja, das ist richtig.

Germans know we are blessed and we thank Gott im Himmel for the wonders of the German Paradise. Mallorca is simply spitze!

The most popular activity in the German Paradise is sun-bathing. Ja, das ist richtig. Everybody loves to bathe in the sun. The glorious sun is there to bathe every German.

There is nothing like sun-bathing in the German Paradise. It's glorious. The sun is just right, like a bathwater carefully controlled by a neurotic woman who has a bath-ritual every day and knows what perfection is in regards to all things relating to bathing.

And there is no dearth of sun-bathing in the German Paradise.

Pleasures of sun-bathing is self-explanatory to those who have participated in the mysteries. It makes your toes curl, so to speak. Ja, das ist richtig.

As you lie on the sandy beach you feel the warmth of sun's hand gently stroking your naked back like a trained masseuse. You feel your body conditioned and sensitized through a natural process.

You feel your body heating up with the passage of every second as if your sensitive areas are gently pressured by a trained hand. As one plus one is two, you feel your body experiencing new levels of elation as you are slowly ushered into the mysteries of sun-bathing.

Some German fraulein like the hard and intense approach to sun-bathing. Instead of pressing their cute, little hiney on fluffy sand, they prefer the hard, heated concrete floor for sun-bathing.

Ja, it may have something to do with being German. Some German fraulein like it hard and intense in the sun-bathing process.

It's like wanting to collide with the mysteries of sun-bathing head-on. It's like saying, "Take me here and now on the burning concrete floor. I want the sun now. Call me Miss Vain!" Ja, das ist richtig.

It's not like they are impatient. That they cannot wait for the sun-bathing to start with prelude leading to climax and ending with a cuddle. But sometimes, the barbarian Germanic tribe past comes through in the fast-and-furious approach to sun-bathing that can be found among some German fraulein.

But by in large, most German fraulein like sunbathing on the glorious sand.

Miles and miles of sand in the German Paradise are covered by countless numbers of sun-bathers who want to be initiated into the mysteries of the German Paradise.

You can tell that these sun-bathers are content and satiated. Sun-bathing can rejuvenate.

But even sun-bathers do not escape the world. Modern times have seen modern amenities on the beach. People use their PDAs, handheld computer games, and cell phones.

It could be annoying, but often those who use them are beautiful sun-bathers that your complaint gets absorbed in the harmony of nature.

Despite the evidence toward modernization and digitization of the sun-bathers, there are still the traditionalists, who prefer to read a newspaper or a book.

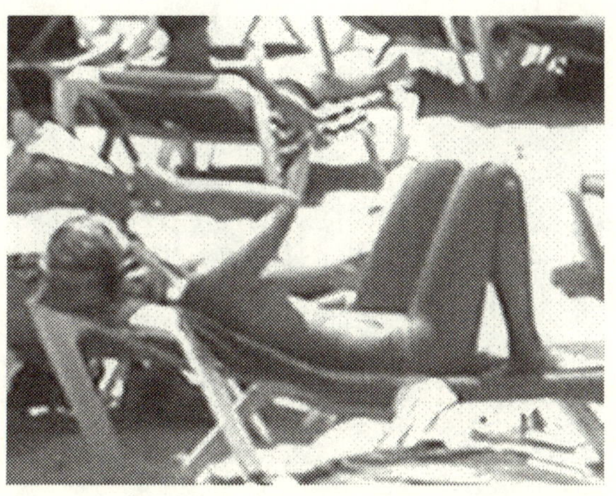

Ja, Paradise Beach is spitze! Water sports, sunbathing, just bumming around, appreciating the creation of Gott im Himmel are all wonderful things to do.

Whenever I think about the German Paradise and the Paradise Beach, I feel like shouting, "Gott sei Dank!"

Ja, a visit to the German Paradise and partaking of the

mysteries of the Paradise Beach is a must. Ja, das ist richtig!

Paradise Party

Ja, Paradise Beach is spitze! Das ist richtig! But the German Paradise would not be complete without the fantastic party scene. I would like to call the party scene, "Paradise Party."

It's no surprise and you would agree that the term is completely appropriate. Ja, das ist richtig.

There is a lot of partying and we Germans like to play hard. Our typical motto is, ""Work hard and play hard." And we Germans feel bound to this motto, and we try to achieve it to the best of our abilities.

The most visible, and perhaps the most popular party spot is Megarena, so visible from the beach promenade.

Megarena is not simply a night spot. In fact, it's open during the day and hundreds of people can be founding drinking beer and enjoying their day programs, which includes wet T-shirt contests to foam dancing in the pool.

But it is in night time that Megarena comes alive with beer guzzling, German sprouting youth. And I tell you, it is a sight to behold.

Ja, I am German, but even I get surprised by the general attractiveness of the population. It appears that non-Germans nearly go nuts when they see all the beautiful German fraulein.

You have to forgive my constant pride-taking at our women, but I am convinced they are superior, so please homor this proud German and don't get to pissed when I go on and on about German fraulein.

Ja, German fraulein are great, and to the joy of many people, the usual composition seems to be that there are more women to men at Megarena and other nightspots.

And Megarena is a fun place to be. They have gigantic drink containers that make the partying more fun and interesting. It certainly serves as a conversation piece.

Ladies seem to like the little nice touches that make the place interesting.

It's almost like paying homage to the libation deity. Festive party atmosphere with German music is just wonderful.

Of course, it must be emphasized that it's a German Paradise and waiters and waitresses all speak German. Menus are in German. But if it were not so, it would not be the German Paradise. So, it all makes sense.

Night life is particularly fun if you speak German. You can find many people to practice your German and you may end up finding a tall, leggy blonde German fraulein to help you with more than the German language. Ja, such is the German Paradise.

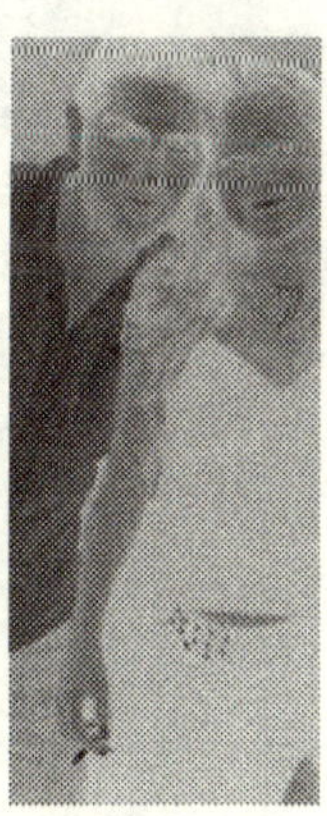

Ja, German fraulein are great and many tend to be really, really friendly as well.

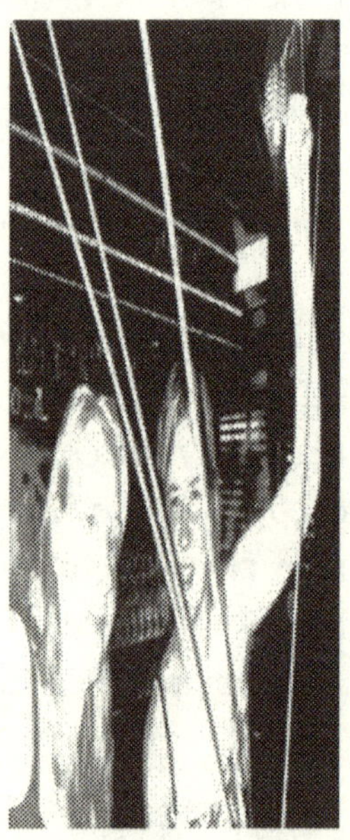

It is the German Paradise for a reason! German fraulein in Mallorca will generally be found in very good spirits and in a partying mood.

But there should be a word of warning. German fraulein have the GWC, remember. This is a very good thing but it can be a bit unnerving as well.

So, let me, as a German dude, give you some advice. The first advice is to learn German.

It is always better to approach German women in their own language. It shows that you are something even though you are not German. Ja, they will think that you are intelligent. And also German fraulein value "making an effort" and speaking in German would qualify as such.

Unlike the French, German fraulein will not be insulted if you butcher the German language. They value your effort and do not expect to be perfect. Even if you feel like a bumbling fool, German fraulein will not treat you as such normally.

A little friendliness goes a long way with German fraulein as with most women. However, a word of warning. German fraulein do not like over-friendliness as a principle.

Especially, there must be warning issued against what I would call "the French method" of starting a conversation.

German fraulein like straightforward, friendly approach the best without too much visible effort or pretension.

One suggestion you can make after saying "hello" is to ask if you can buy them a drink. If they are interested in continuing conversation, they will probably accept. If they are not interested, then they probably will not accept.

German fraulein are straightforward themselves so they will not be shy about telling you what they want or what they do not want.

I presume I should give you some more advice in this regard, lest you fall deeply into a confused mire that permanently disorients you in the dating scene.

Even if a German fraulein accepts your drink, do not assume that the progress will develop in a steady procession. It may do, but it may not do.

Be prepared because generally German fraulein will be quite direct about their sentiments at any point in the conversation. Just assume that the German fraulein believe in the "honesty is the best" policy. So, be prepared emotionally.

Do not be afraid to approach a German fraulein you don't know. Generally, they tend to be good sport about it. They will be direct but usually quite polite about it. So, you should not be too shy.

You should be aware, however, that German fraulein generally like men to be men. In other words, if you look like an artsy-fartsy type of a pretty boy, you probably will not go too far with a German fraulein.

Ja, but this makes sense if you understand the German character. Germans have long been warring tribes and tended to be quite militaristic throughout the whole length of European history.

And remember who started the two world wars. I rest my case. We Germans may not be proud of Hitler and the Nazis, but we are proud of our German strength.

German fraulein have a certain expectation of men. German fraulein want their men to be men, not boys. So, if you look like an artsy-fartsy boy type, you most likely will have no luck in the German Paradise, at least in regards to German fraulein.

Maybe you could find a Dutch girl. Dutch women tend to be a bit more tolerant of the artsy-fartsy factor in men-boys. And there are some running around in the German Paradise.

In fact, there is a Dutch section in the German Paradise. Off in the corner of the beach all way in the end, you'll find Dutch joints.

Germans obviously have the best location because we always tend to be dominant. But the Dutch are nice enough and they don't bother us Germans from enjoying the German Paradise. So, they are all right.

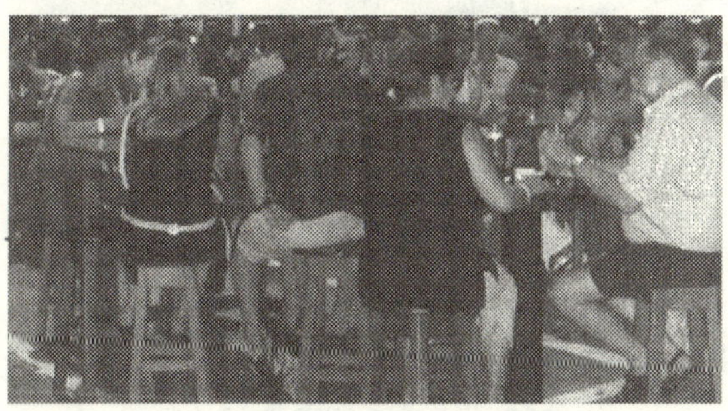

Germans generally like to start drinking in a biergarten setting and end up dancing the night away.

Germans are very active people. Particularly, German fraulein are not the ones to sit around doing nothing.

Most clubs tend to have some live acts and that makes the transition from drinking in a biergarten setting to dancing to rigorous beats a smooth one.

However, you must be aware that the performances will generally be in German. It is the German Paradise after all.

Since the singing can be appreciated without necessarily understanding the language, performances are entertaining for non-German speakers.

However, don't be surprised if you don't clap at the right time or laugh at the same jokes. You have to understand the German language and

German culture to participate in the group setting.

Some non-Germans find German party settings intimidating. Often, unlike American or English party settings, German party setting tend to show a group solidarity that is reminiscent of German stereotypes as a powerful, unified people.

Don't let German group solidarity scare you - unless, of course, you have a reason to be afraid. Germans tend to be quite nice and polite. Unless you go out of your way to make Germans feel like horse doodoo, you have nothing to fear.

One thing that you will notice in German party settings is that Germans like to sing. It maybe the biergarten factor. But we Germans like to sing particularly German songs.

You should not be surprised to find yourself in the middle of a choral type singing of most of the Germans in the room. We will sing and we will sing loudly, given the chance. It is a part of the way we party.

We particularly like German pop songs, but you will also find us singing German folk songs, which are generally described as beer songs in America.

It may be a good idea to try to learn a song or two which get repeated over and over again. Usually, there is two to three songs that Germans love to sing. And we will sing it more than once every night. That makes things easier for you, nein?

Showing appreciation for German culture goes a long way. Germany has a long tradition of pride in all things German.

Germans love being German even though we may never admit to it. So, if you show a little appreciation for German things, you are bound to make many new friends. And some of these new friends may be beautiful German fraulein.

And there are so many gorgeous German fraulein in the German Paradise that the possibilities are endless. Ja, you can experience a bit of heaven on earth. Das ist richtig.

What you will particularly like about German fraulein is that even the most gorgeous will not be very pretentious. You know warum?

It's because there are so many attractive fraulein in Germany that just because you are attractive, you won't think too highly of yourself.

The result is that many attractive German fraulein are really nice and sweet.

It's always a good idea to start Paradise Party early. Certainly by 8:30 PM, you should be buzzing about and being friendly. And Paradise Party can go all night long until 5 AM.

The important thing is to have fun and enjoy the German Paradise.

There is a lot to do. A lot of fun is there to be had, so go out and seize it!

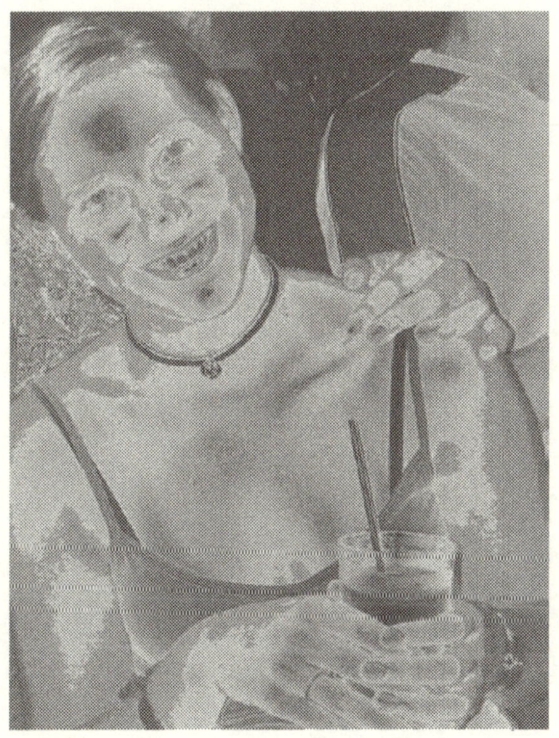

Paradise Exploration

There is a lot to explore in the German Paradise besides your favorite Paradise Beach spot and Paradise Party.

For one, you can go and explore various areas of the coast-line. There are some quaint interesting spots that you will never get to see if you slip out of your bed and walk a few feet to your typical spot on the sandy beach side.

Visiting other parts of the coastline can enrich your experience. You can discover interesting shops, stores, and restaurants. You may even meet some pleasant people in the process.

There are several ways to get around the coastline. For short distances, walking may not be a bad idea.

Wear your swimming trunks so that you will be able to hop into the waters to cool yourself whenever it gets too hot walking. After all, you are walking along the coast-line, so take advantage of it.

There are other ways to keep cool, of course. One recommended advice is to hop into a café for a nice cold drink.

One of the greatest things about enjoying a cold drink in a café is that you are in the shade and probably will have a great view of the coastline.

You can take the opportunity to write a postcard to your friends and share the joys of the German Paradise. You can write about the funny German fraulein that you met the night before. You can pour out your stories of triumphs to your best friends back home. Find ways to entertain yourself. This is a vacation after all.

Your friends will appreciate your deciding to entertain yourself by sharing your stories with them via post, giving a picture of your experience.

Walking definitely can have its rewards. But I understand that you may feel too lazy to walk. After all, it's a vacation right? And walking could feel like a chore, especially on a scorching hot day.

There is a solution for you, of course. You can opt to take a scenic, tourist tram ride along the coast-line road.

Ja, these tourist trams come around once every 15 minutes or so. And it's fun watching people pass by. Often, cute German fraulein ride these trams, so if you position yourself well, you may even make some friends and be able to spend some fun evening with them. Ja, it's all up to you, dude.

A convenient thing about these trams is that you can practically get off whenever you want along the coast.

So, if you see an interesting café, just hop off. If you see a hot German babe who may be the love of your life, then by all means jump off with the zeal of the mad pigs which dashed to the waters when Jesus sent the evil spirits upon them.

The vast road is before you. And a lot can happen on a simple tram ride. It's definitely a fun way to explore the vast coastline.

Do make journey into corner shops and do some serious eye shopping. There are really interesting stores that you will not see back home.

There are special stores that sell Spanish goods. You can locate novelty items. There is a plethora of beach goods, such as inflatables and sports paddles and such. You can pick up sports shirts for cheap as well. Certainly, you can remember to buy that gift for your favorite aunt. Even if she's erratic, and it's difficult to shop for her back home, they'll probably have something along the promenade. Kill a few birds with one stone. Ja.

And what may please you is that items generally tend to cost less than in America and Germany. So, you could pick up a great item for less and have the bragging rights to tell about it at parties back home. It's like bringing a piece of the German Paradise back home with you.

Besides walking into stores, you can try something more rebellious.

There are so many good hotels around and they have interesting pools and, more importantly, different people from those you are used to at your hotel.

You can engage in a drive-by dip. That is, drive-by pool dip.

This is how it works. Just spot a hotel that looks interesting or dull. It doesn't really matter. Find a hotel that you feel comfortable with.

Casually walk inside to the hotel and act like you belong there. Then walk towards the pool. Generally, there are signs so it should not be difficult to spot once you are inside the hotel.

The important thing is not to look nervous. Don't look like you just got out of a big Thanksgiving feast, where you consumed three servings of turkey, swallowed 3 pies, and had cups after cups of apple cider.

Ja, you have to have that look that proclaims, "I know I belong here, and I am proud." Or this look can work as well - "I know what I want and I want it now. Just call me the dude of the German Paradise!"

Nonchalantly walk towards the swimming pool. Grab a beach chair, put your stuff down. Strip down to your swimming trunks and take a plunge in the pool.

It will be an adventure of your making. Just taking a dip in the pool will be success enough.

If you actually engage a cute German babe in a conversation, then you are the dude of the German Paradise.

You will remember this experience for a long time.

And the risk factor isn't so bad. Let's say you get caught doing the drive-by dip. What's the worst that can happen to you?

Maybe the hotel management will ask you to leave? Heck, that'll make you a total rebel. And you know how much chicks dig rebels.

You can spot nice hotels from the tourist tram that you are on and you can hop off as soon as you spot the one that you like.

There are other ways to travel around the area besides the tourist tram, which may actually be more conducive to a possible drive-by pool dip adventure.

You can explore what is the best mode of transportation for you to explore the area.

What's important is that you have fun in the process. You are on vacation for God's sakes and you should not have unnecessary stress. Just go with your first impulse - no thinking, just do. Ja?

Why confine yourself to the local area? You can take a bus or a taxi and explore the city of Palma. It's an interesting city after all and there's quite a bit to see and do there.

I personally prefer to ride the bus because I have had good experience of meeting interesting people. There are vacationers and sometimes they are happy to share their stories with you.

People on vacation tend to be friendlier than people who are not. Ja, das ist richtig. And that includes gorgeous fraulein. Ja?

Bus number 15 is the bus that gets filled up quickly with tourists going to the city of Palma.

It's a short ride - around 30 minutes from the farthest end to the city center. Sometimes, the bus does get overcrowded. If you don't want to get on one bus. The next bus will come in like 15 minutes, so there is really no stress. Ja, you are on vacation to have fun. And the German Paradise is there for you. Ja!

The best place to get off is the bus stop near the sculpture pictured above. When you see the skeleton-looking sculpture, hop off. You will be smack in the middle of the city.

There are obviously quite a lot to do. One thing you may enjoy doing is watching a movie. The movie theater is about one block away from the bus stop of the metal skeleton.

Unfortunately, the movies are all in Spanish. Hey, don't knock it, man. It is Spain after all.

But if you don't understand Spanish, you don't under Spanish. Ja? Still it can be fun watching the movie in a completely another language. You can try to follow the plot just from the pictures. It can be quite a fun experience.

The movie theater is nicely air-conditioned, so there is an added incentive. And the movie ticket price is quite reasonable.

After watching a movie, you can take a break and recover from mental exertion at a nearby café.

Cola can rejuvenate you and give you energy to explore the offerings of the city.

Palma is a fun city, which mixes the old with the new. You can't miss various classic buildings and sculptures.

Like all of Spain, there are very interesting churches in the city. It can be fun to hop inside and explore the paintings and sculptures.

Maybe a friendly priest will be nearby to give you some information about the church's history.

And if you haven't gone to confessions in a while, it can actually even give you that opportunity as well. Kill several birds with one stone, I say. Ja.

There are lots of nice churches to be sure. And like other parts of Spain, there are also nice big squares where you can just chill. Ja, das ist gut!

Stop by to appreciate the sculptures. Or you can appreciate them as you pass by. The sculptures from the past all add to the ambiance of the city.

As I have said, Palma is a city which mixes the old with the new. Perhaps, this is best seen in the ad lib performances during weekends. People casually come together just to have fun and socialize. It's very Spanish, really. And anyone on vacation may enjoy the free spirit and may even learn a dance or two.

It's incredible what you can learn during vacation time if you just put in a little effort.

Memorable vacations happen because you are active in your passivity.

You don't want to stress yourself out with worries and pressured decision-making, but you can allow yourself to explore new areas and new things. Being open to what is out there can enrich your experience and your fun.

It's all about attitude. Ja, das ist richtig.

If you are resolved that you are open to having fun, then you will. If you are open to experiencing the German Paradise to it's fullest, you will. It is simple as that. Das ist richtig!

That is why being open to Spanish culture and Catalan experiences is an important part of experiencing the German Paradise.

In a sense, this accords well with the German mentality. Germans have always been open to experiencing new things.

After all, you are talking about people who descended from proud, warring, "barbarian" tribes.

Our ancestors were fearless. They travelled over vast areas in search of their dreams.

When the Germanic tribes found something that impressed them, they had the openness and the humility to learn from it. And that is what made the German Volk great. And I am very proud to be a part of that heritage.

So, it is natural that the German Paradise will have many things German but also allow open experiences from various other cultures.

Ja, it is the combination of these forces that make Mallorca the German Paradise. And I hope you will consider celebrating the German Paradise with us!

www.ingramcontent.com/pod-product-compliance
Lightning Source LLC
LaVergne TN
LVHW091005080826
845145LV00003B/1137

* 9 7 8 1 5 9 6 8 9 0 0 3 9 *